Life

Everlasting

Finding true fulfilment
through The Apostles' Creed

Life
Everlasting

Finding true fulfilment through The Apostles' Creed

Patricia
St. John

Originally published as
A Missionary Muses on the Creed

CHRISTIAN FOCUS

"Life Everlasting. A Better Way to Live." Originally published as "A Missionary muses on the Creed"Copyright © 1964 Patricia St. John. First published 1964 by Pickering & Inglis Ltd.

Reprinted 2007

ISBN: 978-184550-248-5

Published by Christian Focus Publications Ltd, Geanies House, Fearn, Tain, Ross-shire, IV20 1TW, Scotland, Great Britain.

www.christianfocus.com

email:info@christianfocus.com

Cover design by Danie van Straaten

Printed and Bound in Denmark

by Norhaven Paperback A/S.

www.christianfocus.com

Contents

Introduction 7

The Apostles' Creed............................. 13

I believe in God the Father................... 15

I believe in Jesus Christ his only Son... 23

I believe in the Holy Spirit................... 29

I believe in the Holy catholic church... 39

I believe in the communion of saints... 49

I believe in the forgiveness of sins........ 61

I believe in the resurrection 73

Aisha's Letter 83

Patricia St John - her story 91

Introduction

Most of my childhood was spent on the compound of the British Hospital in Tangier where my parents were missionaries with the North Africa Mission (today's Arab World Ministries). My father worked as a radiographer in the hospital and also pastored the English-speaking church on the compound while my mother ran a junior school.

Patricia St. John was a major figure in my life during those years when she both worked as a nurse in the hospital and also did clinics in the remote Riff Mountains town of Chauen about eighty miles away. It is Chauen, a holy place of pilgrimage for Muslims, its buildings all whitewashed, that is referred to constantly in the pages of this book.

Today, adults would label Patricia as 'a loose cannon' since she was not under the mission's authority and was free to go anywhere and do anything she felt God was indicating. As children, we adored her, hung on her every word, and crowded round her knowing she would always give in and tell us stories that held us spellbound.

From those far-off days in the 1950s and 60s came her children's classics Treasures of the Snow, Tanglewoods Secrets, Star of Light and more. Since then, these books have never lost their power to entrance and hold the rapt attention of successive generations of youngsters.

I am glad that this book is being reprinted because it keeps us in touch with one of the 20th century's most fascinating and able missionary saints. It is not going too far to say that Patricia St. John was to many of us a living example of Christ himself for she loved us all, but especially her Moroccan friends, with a love so transparently like his.

The poem on the following pages is one by Patricia St. John that has not been previously published. It was written for me as an encouragement when I left Tangier to start nurse training at St. Thomas's Hospital, London, where Patricia herself trained. I had told her one of my favourite Bible verses was Psalm 16:11 and she handed me the poem as a farewell gift.

Yvonee Fyles

Hilton of Cadboll

Ross-shire

Enter thou into the joy of the Lord,

For I am the door!

Why do you sit in the gloom of the prison?

The sun o'er the ramparts is newly arisen

And fountains well up from their rock-hidden sources

Till the streams, merry silver, are flooding their courses,

And the fair path of life lies unshadowed before you

And I am the door.

I am the door to all sunshine and laughter,

All love and delight!

Yet how strong is the foe that is waiting to rout us,

The small jealous terrors that weave chains about us;

No daylight can enter self's fortified city

Or pierce through those windowless walls of self-pity,

And deep are our dungeons of pride and resentment

Yet I am the door

By my Cross and my tomb I passed through the prison

And opened the door.

My pierced hands can loosen the grave-clothes

that bind you,

Step over the threshold and leave them

behind you!

How fearful you cringe in the darkness you cherish,

But my life is your freedom, come forth ere you perish,

The light that you dread shall but gladden

and guide you

And Christ is the door.

Patrica St. John

The Apostles' Creed

I believe in God the Father Almighty,
creator of Heaven and Earth.
I believe in Jesus Christ,
his only Son,
Our Lord.
He was conceived by the Holy Spirit
He was born of the virgin Mary
He suffered under Pontius Pilate
He was crucified, died and was buried
He descended to the dead
On the third day he rose again
and ascended into heaven
He is seated on the right hand
of God the Father
He will come again to judge
the living and the dead
I believe in the Holy Spirit,
the holy catholic church
The communion of saints
The forgiveness of sins
The resurrection of the body
and the life everlasting.

I believe in God the Father

It was late at night. The missionary was sitting in a small hut on the outskirts of a village in the North African mountains. The hut was lit by an oil lamp and the glow of a fire on which a clay pot bubbled. The air was heavy with the fumes of charcoal, boiling oil and humanity.

All the hostess' friends and relations had crowded in to see the English woman, and she had been proclaiming the Gospel message in rather faltering Arabic to group after group for nearly two hours. Now, tired out and giddy with sleep, she suggested closing down.

'But the night is yet young!' cried her disappointed audience, 'and the partridge is not yet cooked. Tell us one more story!' They sat cross-legged, smiling ingratiatingly, their dark eyes gleaming in the firelight.

The missionary turned in despair to the young woman who sat beside her and who had walked over the hills with her that afternoon. Her name was Fatima, and only a few months before she had come out of Islam and accepted Christ. She was a loving, true Christian, but illiterate, ignorant and very shy. She had led the missionary to many villages, but she had never yet spoken in public.

'Will you speak to them?' asked the missionary, and she knew she was asking no light thing. To confess Christ openly among her own people might mean bitter persecution.

But Fatima was ready. There was one story which had always meant more to her than any other, and she launched forth into the parable of the lost sheep, adding a wealth of local detail, for she herself was of shepherd stock. The villagers sat transfixed. While the missionary spoke, they had listened as children listen to a story – laughing and interrupting. But this was one of their own people; their faces became shrewd and cautious, the atmosphere silent and tense.

'Now tell me this,' asked the speaker, as the story drew to a triumphant close, 'why did that shepherd go out all night to look for that sheep? He was a rich man and he had ninety-nine others. What made him go?

'Then I will tell you,' she said at last. 'He went to look for that sheep because he could not rest till his flock was complete. All his heart that night was with that missing lamb… and that is why we have come tonight. The Lord has many Christians in other countries, and there are Christians of this land; but he is not satisfied. He wants the people of Benilzeed and Beni Hamid and Magree. He cannot rest till his flock is complete.'

She swept her hand across the open doorway, where across the valley the lights of other villages twinkled like clusters of stars in the hollows of the dark mountains. The villagers nodded thoughtfully, and the missionary leaned against the wall, weary but satisfied: a poor, ignorant, illiterate woman, yet surely she had known the Father.

St. John, in his Epistle, ascribes two characteristics to his little children: their sins are forgiven and they have known the Father and without this knowledge there seems to be no promotion (I John 2:12-13). To know the Father means to know the heart of the Father, which can never rest until his family is complete; which yearns over every separate prodigal, and gives all its love to each wayward individual. An earthly father who loses a child can never again look at the group of living sons and daughters without seeing the gap. Each one, present or absent, has all his heart.

'He that hath seen me hath seen the Father,' said Christ. Hanging on the cross, he was bearing away the sin of the world. Yet all his heart was with one dying thief.

This knowledge, according to John, is fundamental. It is one of the first revelations that God gives to his 'little children', yet in the rush and hurry of the modern missionary life there is, perhaps, no truth more easily forgotten. We enlarge our organizations, and we must fix rigid routines, which must be got through in time; we thank God for the increased opportunities of coming in contact with the masses, but we recognise the dangers. We know the irritation we may feel toward the awkward individual who puts a spoke in the wheel, or interrupts, or claims our attention at the wrong moment, and how we may hurry on fuming, utterly blind to the intrinsic worth of that individual and with a heart a million miles away from the heart of the Father.

Perhaps nothing more emphasizes the gulf that existed between Christ and his disciples than their reaction to interruptions and their attitude toward individuals who claimed the Lord's attention at some inconvenient moment or in some unconventional way. The disciples felt there was only one thing to be done with a crowd of women and small children who interrupted the preaching – to get them out of the way as soon as possible. But this was not the attitude of the one who came to reveal the Father. The disciples saw a lot of annoying children underfoot, but he saw his own kingdom and laid his hands on each individual little one – 'Take heed that ye despise not one of them,' he said.

'Send her away,' said the disciples indignantly as the Canaanite woman followed them screaming. To them she was a badly behaved, embarrassing woman, defying their conventions. To him she was one of the broken hearts he had come to heal.

'Send the multitudes away!' cried the tired twelve, exasperated by the crowds. To them, a rabble of sightseers who had broken in on their hardly-earned rest; to him, 5,000 separate sheep each needing a Shepherd.

How far have we believed in God the Father and pondered the real meaning of our belief? We are thankful for the big missionary organisation, the mass movements. But may God give us to look on them not as crowds that have got to be dealt with somehow, but as lost souls over whom the heart of the Father yearns and suffers, and if we cannot do this, then may God keep us from them for we shall only misrepresent the Gospel we came to preach. May we so believe in the Father, and so stand identified with our belief, that somewhere behind the evil rags, or the demanding rudeness, or the awkward, unconventional behaviour of any specific individual we may see blazoned the supreme value of the human soul – 'A brother or sister for whom Christ died.'

I believe in Jesus Christ his only Son

They were sitting on the hillside together in the clear autumn sunshine, the older missionary troubled and perplexed, the younger language student voicing her indignation. The slopes round them were still cracked dry clods, for though the first rains had fallen, they had as yet made little impression.

'It just seems to be the general attitude,' cried the language student bitterly. 'Old Miss Smith[1] said to me the other day, "It's no good trusting any of them." But how can we win them and help them unless we are willing to trust them? Doesn't it say that love believeth all things?'

[1] Fictional names used.

'Yes,' answered the older missionary, 'it does. And certainly the more we can trust, the more likely people are to become trustworthy. And yet…' She fell silent, looking back over her ten years of service, and the hard, painful, humiliating path that lay behind her of learning not to trust.

She knew that every young enthusiastic idealist who ever gets down to grips with life as it really is in any country with a Christless religion would have to tread the same path. No one can avoid it except those who deliberately choose to wrap themselves up in unreality. But must the gradual shattering of a young missionary's eager, loving belief in human nature inevitably lead to cynicism, dreary disappointment and consequent uselessness and unlove? What is the other destination to which it could lead?

A number of little incidents rose before her mind. She could think about them dispassionately now, but they had been bitter enough at the time. She remembered the young man who professed to have been cast out of his village for the sake of the Gospel, on whom an over-worked missionary had spent many precious hours of prayer and teaching

— until the young man disappeared, and so did the missionary's only overcoat. She thought of the evangelist who had made an appeal at the end of a gospel meeting for boys and had asked to see separately all those who raised their hands. Quite a group queued up in that little passage and it was only later that the owner of the house discovered that not a single spoon or knife was left in the little cupboard beside which the 'new converts' had waited. She could laugh now at the endless ways in which her own simplicity and naivety had been exploited, but she had not laughed at the time. It was not easy learning to mistrust.

'Love believeth all things.' Were those words just beautiful but unpractical, or was there another interpretation that could bring everything into focus?

The woman on the hillside suddenly remembered a letter that had reached her a few days previously from a girl born a Muslim, but converted to Christianity at the age of seventeen. Every early step of the way had been fiercely contested, for the devil knows how to fight for such souls; but she had battled through and after five years training she was about to enter Bible school preparatory to returning as a missionary midwife to her own people.

'I am about to start on a new life,' she wrote, 'and I feel a little afraid. But when I look back on the way he has led me I can only believe…'

Believe in what? In the weak base clay of human nature, or in the hands that have taken hold of it? In a Christless country even a regenerate man may take years to shed entirely the habits and customs and trend of thought of a lifetime. To trust even in the true convert is often to doom oneself to bitter cynical disappointment, and to harm him by one's own reaction. To believe that all things are possible to the hands that have taken hold of him, to look with the eyes of the potter and to see in the yet ugly lump the vessel that may be is the sure antidote for any breakdown in love or faith. That hand has never broken a bruised reed or cast away a smoking flax or given up a failing saint, because the Lord knows the strength of his own love.

'All they which are in Asia be turned away from me,' wrote Paul to Timothy; but according to Bishop Moule we can translate verse twelve of that same chapter, 'Nevertheless I am not the least disappointed, for I know whom I have believed.' Love accepts reality, sees human nature as it is, but believes that all things are possible to God, and joyfully strong in that assurance, continues to hope all things of the most hopeless because the Saviour has not given up; endures all things, all disappointment and all ingratitude, believing in the unwearied love of Christ; never fails, because he shall not fail nor be discouraged.

'We cannot always believe in people, even in Christian people,' answered the older missionary slowly. 'But we can believe in the Lord Jesus Christ. It is the only foundation for any stable love; not what they are, but what he can make them.'

They fell silent. The sun burned down relentlessly on the parched ground; it was a lifeless scene at first sight. But a crocus had sprung up through a cracked furrow, and not far away a cluster of dwarf narcissi scented the hot air. It seemed a miracle that such frail beauty could have pierced such drought, but who can fathom the power of life? There are miracles round us every day. A casual glance sees only the hard soil, but the seeker finds a flower and, pausing to consider, can only say, 'I believe in Jesus Christ.'

I believe in the Holy Spirit

It was 8.30 in the evening and the hospital evangelist glanced at his watch and gathered up his paraphernalia with a rather tired sign – the piano accordion, the hymn books, and the few Gospels to be given away to any readers who asked for them. But tonight no one had asked, and most of the men appeared half asleep. There was a desperately ill case of typhoid who kept crying out, and a convalescent patient who resolutely and definitely murmured his Muslim prayers during the service. The evangelist had sung the same old hymns by himself that night, and preached to an audience huddled, for the most part, under the blankets. It was not always like that by any means. Sometimes they all sat up and took notice, and in the tubercular ward upstairs where the men stayed for months at a time there was usually earnest attention, with occasional conversation. But in the acute surgical ward the patients came and went so quickly; it was hard to believe that much could penetrate in so short a time, especially when, to begin with, they were often oblivious to all but their pain.

'So is the Kingdom of God, as if a man should cast seed into the ground; and should sleep and rise night and day, and the seed should spring and grow up, he knoweth not how. For the earth bringeth forth fruit of itself...'

Eighty miles away up in the mountains a young missionary was running a dispensary. It was market day, and the dim little room was packed with brown, bearded tribesmen from the villages around. They looked healthy enough, but some had teeth broken by the village barber and wanted roots extracted, and others wanted ointment for cracked leathery feet. All were in a hurry to start back on the long hot climb home, and the young missionary who always started with a Gospel message knew that she must be short and concise. She opened her book and started to read a passage.

The moment she mentioned the name of Jesus a rough unshaven man in an orange turban leaped to his feet and turned on the audience: 'I know about him,' he cried excitedly. 'Down in the hospital… a man came and played and sang… he said that as Moses lifted up the serpent in the wilderness even so must the Son of Man be lifted up… He did a great, great deed… He died for us.' Then turning to the missionary he asked eagerly, 'Tell me, where can I get that book that tells about that man?'

'If you will wait to the end,' replied the missionary, 'I will give you one.'

So he waited till the room was empty, and then came forward. He had been in the mission hospital some eighteen months before for some minor complaint, and had only stayed five days. On later enquiry it transpired that neither the medical staff nor the evangelist remembered him. Shy and inarticulate, he had said nothing to betray his interest. But on one of those five nights he had heard the third chapter of John's Gospel, and the Holy Spirit had worked.

Who else could have convinced that illiterate, ignorant man that Jesus had really been lifted up on a cross? The Muslims deny it, but Abdulla, alone of all his tribe, believed it. His life was hard, and he had much to think about. His little strip of land was baked hard by the heat; the price of corn was going up. He must plough and sow, and walk eighteen miles to market and back over high rocky mountains, at least once a week. Yet a year and a half after hearing of that death by crucifixion, he still knew that it was a matter of tremendous importance to him.

He came for weeks on end. His village was almost wholly illiterate and he could find no one to read with him there. But he listened to page after page of the Gospel story, and on being asked, 'Do you believe that Jesus is the Son of God?' he replied, 'If I did not believe, would I walk all this way over the mountains to hear about him?' Sometimes he combined his visits with market business, sometimes he just came to hear more. Then he found a reader in the village, and joyfully took a Gospel home with him. And after that he disappeared.

It is often so in missionary work, especially among scattered country tribes. The missionary who waited week after week for his return will probably never know whether he was dissuaded or threatened, or whether something happened to him. She might say sadly, 'Just another bright beginning that came to nothing,' or she might say, 'I believe in the Holy Spirit.' For the seed is being planted and God himself has made seeds with intricate devices for being scattered very far. The winged sycamore fruit and the tiny parachute of the dandelion may germinate miles from the parent plant. A seed may also lie dormant for many years and then some new condition of growth or some gleam of sunlight may release the latent life. The Holy Spirit brooded over the waste and confusion and darkness of the earth, and he still bides his time as he broods over the living seed dropped into the chaos and darkness of a human heart.

'He would make an excellent evangelist,' said one, of a young man blessed with a persuasive, arresting manner of speech and a tactful, imaginative approach. These are certainly useful qualities, but there are others more necessary, and there are two that are essential.

The first is patient obedience. Jesus has told us to preach the Gospel, and the habit of obedience is sometimes the only incentive to go on. The love of Christ constrains us, but the mind that gives itself unstintingly, day after day, to preaching the Gospel in a foreign language is often exhausted of any feeling of emotion, and is not always conscious of any compelling urge of love. At those times, the evangelist can only measure the reality of his love by the standard that Jesus gave us: 'If you love me keep my commandments.' And so he goes on preaching.

The second is faith in the Holy Spirit and in nothing else. The servants who drew the water at the wedding knew that no touch of theirs could change it to wine. Theirs the routine work of carrying buckets, but they knew that the Lord was at the wedding, and the moment came when he stretched out his hand and the dull labour was crowned, and the wine sparkled in the water pots, (John 2). Jehosophat's soldiers who dug the trenches all through the night did not know what would happen, (II Kings 3). Their part was to lift the cold clay, their eyes heavy with sleep, and they went on digging and irrigating until the sun rose, and the miracle of victory took place. And without that faith in the fact that our missionary routine is merely a preparation for that transforming touch, and never an end in itself, few would be foolish enough to start pitting their little speeches against the overwhelming strength of unbelief.

So day after day the evangelist tells out the same message, with various degrees of emotion to the same unresponsive crowds. Occasionally he will see a conversion, but in the natural world seeds do not grow the day they are planted. Sometimes he will preach to people who, as far as he knows, he will never see again, and one face, usually that of a woman, will light up with a sudden yearning understanding. But there is no one free to follow up that woman or to teach her more. Can that flicker or light survive, or will it immediately be extinguished by the darkness around it? 'The Holy Spirit shall teach you all things... He shall take of mine and shew it to you.'

Far among rocks and hills
Have I planted my seed;
In the dust and drought under sun-baked clod,
Where the foot of a sower never trod,
In the crumbled furrows where birds of prey
Hidden in clefts in the heat of the day,
Swoop at even to snatch the shoot
Of the living seed that has cast its root;
Where crackling creeper and leafless thorn
Strangle the life of a blade new-born,
And the sower's labour is laughed to scorn,
I have planted my seed.

Unto the Spirit of Life
I commit my seed.
Now will I rise and go my way.
To the stars by night and the sun by day,
To the drought and the dew
and the Autumn rain
I yield my treasure of scattered grain.
With tired hands and a trembling faith
I fling my seed to the wastes of death;
Scattered so far, I shall never know
How much may perish, how much may grow,

Nor of secret stirrings 'neath frost and snow
In the buried seed.

Power of Risen Life shall quicken my seed;
Life that is born of God's own breath,
Stronger than winter or drought or death.
Scattered, stunted, blighted at birth,
Yet each living seedling of matchless worth
To the Lord, who shall life them
from fields of time
And transplant them far in a sweeter clime,
Where in love's own soil
they shall cast their root
And his life shall quicken the shrivelled shoot,
And each branch, abiding, shall bear its fruit
Through the life of God.

I believe in the
Holy catholic church

An enthusiastic visiter to the mission hospital asked, 'And into what denomination do you baptise your converts?'

'Converts from Islam are few and far between,' replied the missionary, 'and they know nothing about denominations. We baptize them in the name of the Father, the Son, and the Holy Spirit, and they become members of the Christian Church.'

'Oh, but isn't that rather complicated?' asked the visitor doubtfully. 'For instance, what denomination do your nurses and doctors belong to?'

The missionary considered a moment. 'I'm really not sure,' she replied. 'I know of two who worship with the Brethren in England, and a couple of American Baptists, and there is at least one who belongs to the Church of England; but I've never asked the rest. We seem to lose interest in that kind of thing out here and besides, we could hardly pronounce them all if we knew them. Last Sunday at the bilingual Easter service, in a congregation composed mainly of missionaries and national Christians there were over ten different nationalities represented. The three who were led to come forward at the end to administer the Lord's Supper happened to be a Jew, a Gentile, and an Arab respectively.

'But what form of church worship do you adopt?' asked the visitor.

Again the missionary had to think. 'There is no set form of worship laid down,' she answered at length. 'The churches, such as they are, are very small, sometimes a mere handful of women and children and at present they usually meet in the missionary's house. The form of service is probably slightly coloured by the home affiliations of the

one in charge, but we try to let the little gathering give natural expression to the ideas of the local Christians.'

'I suppose this just applies to your mission society?' queried the visitor. 'I suppose there are other agencies who have other methods working in the country.'

'There are about seven agencies working among the indigenous people of the country,' answered the missionary, 'and two have recently joined up, three are inter-denominational, and the rest draw their members from one denomination. But we are particularly fortunate in the fact that they are all evangelical by conviction, and in the consequent unity that exists among them. Two conferences for national Christians are held each year in which converts resulting from the labours of all agencies unite, and the speakers are drawn from all or any. The summer camps for children are run on the same basis, and the big annual missionary prayer conference is a gathering to which every missionary is welcome, and at which reports of all the work are given and prayed over. One group serves all the others by sending out free Bible correspondence courses, and the literature committee and the Bible translation committee are inter-agency affairs. Probably very few national Christians are aware of any difference between us.'

'Well, I suppose it ought to be like that,' said the visitor, 'but I did not know that such a state of affairs existed.'

The conversation veered off on to other subjects, but the missionary continued to ponder a situation she had hitherto taken for granted, and her thoughts flew back to a thin sickly boy with an enormous ulcer on his leg who had visited her day after day up in the mountains. He had heard something about the Lord every time he had his dressing done, and one morning he had visited her very early, with a troubled look on his face, and shutting and locking the door carefully behind him he drew her into the dispensary and sat down. 'I was sleeping by my loom,' he explained, 'and I had a dream. I thought I saw a long road leading to a cross, and someone was hanging on it – I think it was Jesus, the Christ. And all round the cross there were people waiting to kill me, hiding in the shadows. But behind the cross was an open door, and I knew that if I could reach that cross and enter that open door I would find refuge, and be safe. Can you tell me the meaning of that dream?'

As simply as possible the missionary explained the way of salvation to the boy but she thought about his words long after he had gone back to his weaving. The cross – the world's greatest and bloodiest battlefield, where Satan's most poisoned arrows are being hurled all the time. Only let a soul look toward the cross, and the whole might of hell will be let loose on him to prevent him going further. We have seen it countless times over – the first happy confession of faith, the bright beginning – and then the overwhelming temptation of fear and to sin and to draw back, and the apparent triumph of Satan as yet another 'convert' slips back to Islam.

But behind the cross was an open door and a refuge. Christ never meant his new-born babes to stand alone on that battlefield. He ordained for them a Church. He designed to make them members of his body, drawn into living loving fellowship with other believers, not lone fighters, but one of an army, massed together against an overwhelming and, at present, a conquering foe. In the battle between Christ and Islam the apparent victories of Satan should cause us to mass our forces, stand shoulder to shoulder and fling every ounce of our reserve strength into our central objective.

Yet is it not a fact that some tired, tempted new convert may join our ranks, imagining that we shall stand beside him in the great battle against Satan and sin, only to find that another battle is raging? The ranks themselves are divided. The passion and strength that should have been pitted against the central objective are being wasted on tiny matters of priority or rights, or the to-be-or-not-to-be of ecclesiastical detail. These things can fill our minds to the exclusion of the real foe, and in the end we may find that the fight is no longer for souls, but a fight against each other for our own sectarian or personal standing and recognition.

And what is the result for the convert in the first critical weeks of new birth? He as yet knows very little about the Lord and may be illiterate. The missionary who showed him the way has no doubt taught him the verse, 'By this shall all men know that ye are my disciples, if you have love one for another,' and he watches eagerly for the outworking of this insignia of Christianity. He realises that before the grasp of Islam the movement is weak, but he expects at least to find an internal strength and solidity with which he can ally himself.

A simple country woman who had been the first to believe in her village and had learned from her New Testament and from one isolated missionary for three years, came down to town eager to meet other Christians. But within the first few weeks she was conscious of contention and strain. She walked into her room where her friend was sitting and laid her New Testament down on the table. 'For three years you taught me that Christians loved each other, and I believed you,' she said bitterly. 'Now I know you were deceiving me all the time.' That woman now stands on the border line, neither truly Christian nor truly Muslim. Perhaps some reader will pray for her.

The central insistence of Christ's last recorded prayer for his Church on earth was that they all might be one, because he foresaw that our unity would be, right through the ages, the central point of Satan's attack. The devil can seldom succeed in leading an experienced missionary into open sin, nor can he often stop him fighting, for a missionary is essentially a fighter, but he can subtly divert the warfare into other channels until it becomes almost ineffectual against his own kingdom, and he can rage on unchecked. How often and how easily we persuade ourselves that we are battling for a principle, when we are merely fighting for our own pride and right.

'I believe in the Holy catholic church.' The implication is terrific. It means that we believe in only one true division between light and darkness, death and life. It means that, drawn together by the magnitude of our warfare, each one who loves Christ is putting his all into one objective – the saving of sinners, the building up of the assaulted Church, and the guarding of the threatened flock. If we have the time, thought or strength left for any other fight, then we are detracting from the main issue and weakening the attack. Worst of all the Church of God has ceased to become a refuge of love for the sorely tried convert. He has merely fled for help in the great strife to find himself involved in a bewildering series of lesser strifes.

Can we wonder that the Church is weakened by young Christians who have never even glimpsed the purpose and the struggle to which they have been called? May God keep us single-minded, fighting one foe, marching under one standard, that those who join us may fall into step; and the Church of God may yet be fair as the moon, clear as the sun, terrible as an army with banners.

I believe in the
communion of saints

It was late at night but too hot to sleep; the missionary sat at the open window looking out into the breathless night and thinking back over the past week. She wanted to pray, but prayer did not come easily. Instead she seemed to see the indifferent faces of the patients, to whom she had preached, and heard afresh the passionate voices of two girls who had quarrelled in Bible class.

The frightened eyes of a boy, recently baptised, but caught stealing, flashed in front of her, and the disappointing emptiness of the tea table, when three enquirers, eagerly awaited, all failed to turn up. Depression descended upon her. What was it all leading to? Was it, after all, a mere waste of time?

Then suddenly a verse flashed into her mind and comforted her. The Lord himself had been speaking through the prophet. 'I have laboured in vain, I have spent my strength for nought and in vain.' The Lord himself had felt as she was feeling; she did not have a High Priest who could not be touched with the feeling of her infirmities. And not only could he enter into her disappointment and discouragement, but she, too was beginning to enter into his experiences. It could all become a communion of the closest kind: 'that I may know the fellowship of his suffering.'

It is not given to most of us to enter in any real way into the sufferings of the cross. Few of us missionaries will be called to bear real persecution or to endure physical pain or death for Christ's sake, although Christians in other countries may have to drink of that cup. None of us will ever know anything about that crowning agony of the cross, the averted face of God. But we have not been excluded from the fellowship. The things that must have broken the heart of Christ every day of his three years' ministry are being enacted in our midst all the time. They can either harden us into insensate machines of routine that crash on at all costs, or they can send us home with a nervous breakdown, or they can initiate us daily into a deeper communion with Christ, sharing his sorrow, sharing his reactions, and in the end sharing the triumph of his love.

There is the suffering caused by the carelessness of those around to the things or God, and we know all about that. We know what it is to give time and prayer and careful preparation to a message delivered in the end to an apparently unresponsive audience; to have a meeting completely ruined by four or five babies who cannot possibly be left at home, or to have our Gospel appeal interrupted in the middle of a sentence by a kindly country voice from the audience: 'How much did your stockings cost? … Have you got a husband? … Are your teeth your own?'; to address a crowd who only seem impatient to be done with talking and to get in for their medicine. All this has been known to the Lord. His own solemn discourse on the Holy Spirit was interrupted one day by a voice from the multitude: 'Master, speak to my brother that he divide the inheritance with me.' He was interrupted by little children, but, in each case, instead of giving up in despair as we tend to do, he took up the interruption and turned it into an immortal, spontaneous sermon. He fully realised that in most hearts the cares of the world would choke the word, but he did not stop preaching; for he knew that among the thorns and rocks there were patches of soft earth. In the midst of the stony ground of the ritualists there was Nicodemus. The seed cast so prodigally into the mire of greed and self-seeking that characterized the tax-gatherers reached Levi and Zacchaeus. He sowed lavishly in the mud of the streets and found Mary Magdalene.

There is that satanic sense of opposition that rises up almost imperceptibly in an audience when the tenets of their own religion are challenged; that withdrawal of the mind behind shutters, so that further words seem like the bombardment of a blank wall. The moral refusal has been made, and there is nothing more we can do about it. Perhaps we have ceased to suffer much over it, or perhaps we have settled down into a sort of chronic passive depression. But the Lord never ceased to suffer much over it. 'Ye will not come unto me that ye might have life,' he cried with tears. 'O Jerusalem, Jerusalem ... how often would I have gathered thy children together ... and ye would not!' There was nothing passive about the way Christ accepted their rejection. Such anguish is active and strong, and because of it, 'Israel shall yet be gathered.'

He knows all about the "rice" Christians, too; the poor women who come to the meetings with cold babies and profess deep interest because they think they may get a little woolly. ('I will enter your way if you will promise to clothe my son and find me work,' said one brightly.) Human nature was just the same in Christ's day. Hundreds came to him for merely physical reasons. 'Ye seek me because ye did eat of the loaves,' he said gently to the crowds at Tiberias, and it is interesting to note that he did not condemn them for their ulterior motives. When they were sick he healed them, and when they were hungry he gave them bread; but he always made it clear that he had more to give if they would take it.

'You love our souls but you don't love us,' said a discontented boy of seventeen to a missionary.

That may be true of us, but it could never had been said of the Lord. He loved the body, soul and spirit, and their sickness, fear, and hunger cried to his heart. He wept with Mary; he had compassion on the multitudes. He bore their griefs and carried their sorrows. His call to the heavy laden was not restricted to those bearing spiritual burdens only. It was his sympathy with their human lot that opened their heart to his teaching.

'How did you come to believe in Christ?' asked a missionary of an old, tired water-carrier. The wrinkled face brightened. 'I heard you tell how Jesus said, "Come unto me all ye that labour and are heavy laden, and I will give you rest",' she replied, 'and I said to myself, "That's me with my water buckets!" I started to whisper the name of Jesus whenever I climbed the hill, and my buckets are much lighter than they used to be.' He had met her at her level of need and cared for her aching back and tired arms. Later she learned with joy about those other burdens he would carry for her.

He has felt the hurt caused by ingratitude, but he never became bitter or cynical or stayed his hand because of it. 'Where are the nine?' he asked sadly. 'Did only one trouble to come back and say thank you?' Three years of self-giving to Judas was rewarded by betrayal and, indeed, that pain must pierce his constant loving heart day after day. He continues to send his rain on the just and the unjust and he crowns us with loving kindness and tender mercies. How many of us ever really express our gratitude?

And, lastly, he knows all about the hurt and disappointment of souls born again who fail and fall and miss the highest – converts of whom we hoped so much so often seem to draw back. We may have spent hours with them over the word but there seems little fruit. Fear and a sort of Eastern fatalism blights their purpose, and sometimes we are amazed at the ease with which they revert to the godless habits and customs of their past life, and at their lack of understanding. Often we wonder, is it any good going on teaching them? They need conviction of sin, not teaching.

Yet who were those men to whom Christ committed that last deep teaching of the upper room? They were those who, after Christ had told them of the manner of his death, immediately started quarrelling as to who should be the greatest; who, even on the last night with the shadow of the cross already fallen on them, were each stubbornly refusing to rise up and wash the feet of the others. They were so slow of understanding that after three years with Jesus he still had to say sadly, 'Have I been so long time with you, and yet hast thou not known me?' In spite of all their protestations he knew that they would all forsake him in the course of the next few hours. And yet it was to these men that he entrusted the truth about the Holy Spirit, the deity of Christ, the secret of abiding and the gift of his peace. It was to them that he said, 'I have called you friends.'

Three little phrases perhaps explain the reasons he had for daring to do this.

First, he knew the strength of his own love. 'Having loved his own that were in the world he loved them to the end.'

He had no delusions about these men. He knew exactly what they were, but he had no intention of giving them up. He knew what his constant, dying, living love could make of them. Do we sometimes forget that love, both divine, and the divine expressed through the human, is the strongest transforming power in the world?

Secondly, 'I have many things to say unto you, but ye cannot bear them now. Howbeit when he, the Spirit of truth is come, he will guide you into all truth.'

Christ was doing what every missionary must learn to do, especially in our teaching of children. He was laying the fuel, and one day the Holy Spirit would light the fire. They were not yet ready to put his precepts into practice, but when they were, at least they would know what to do. Thank God for the bright sparks of pentecostal and revival preaching, but the fire they kindle will die out quickly unless there is the solid fuel of Bible teaching on which to feed it. And one usually lays a fire before one lights it.

Thirdly, 'I pray for them.'

Christ knew the keeping power of his own intercession. Before ever he called his disciples he spent all night in prayer to God. He had prayed for Peter, looking far ahead beyond his denial, preparing the way for his restoration. Have we really grasped the power that has been given us to protect and restore our weak, failing little flock? Have we made full use of the weapon of intercessory prayer?

The path of Jesus in this world was a path of apparent disappointment and rejection, and we want to walk with Jesus. No other path brings us so close to him, and we shall never know much of him on this earth except through the fellowship of his sufferings, for that communion opens the door to all other communions. Sharing his suffering we shall begin to share his reaction to suffering, and that character that only came to perfection through suffering.

Perhaps no one has ever expressed it better than the old divine, William Law, who certainly believed in the communion of saints.

'Receive every inward and outward trouble,' he wrote, 'every disappointment, darkness and desolation and pain with both hands, as a true opportunity of entering into fuller fellowship with thy self-denying, suffering Saviour. Look at no inward or outward trouble in any other view, reject every thought about it, and then every kind of trial and distress will become the blessed day of thy prosperity.'

I believe in the forgiveness of sins

The dark-eyed orderly said to the missionary, 'Oh yes, I'm a Christian.' The missionary was trying to discover the cause of his unwillingness to help in evangelistic work.

'But what about the past? I know the missionaries were good to me, and gave me work, but why was I never given a good education? And why am I in this poorly paid job? What chance is there for me to rise in the world now? No, I'm not helping.'

'Well, she seems genuine enough in her desire to start afresh as a Christian,' said the missionary's wife doubtfully, 'but don't forget that I trusted her, and she did go off with three eggs and a roller towel and my toothbrush on different occasions. I know she was young and very poor, but that does not excuse sin. Personally, I'd rather not try again.'

'We disagreed about X at the last committee meeting,' said the evangelist. 'I know X is sincere, and M is certain that he is a hypocrite. We had some words about it, and although we prayed about it afterwards, I've never felt quite the same about M since. We always seem a bit strained with each other.'

'I know I put my foot into it and messed things up at the beginning,' said the second-year recruit bitterly. 'If I could start again with the knowledge and experience I have now, how different things would be! But people don't forget things like that, and they'll never want me now. All I can do is to keep away from them and get on quietly with my own work. Perhaps one day they'll believe that I've changed.'

As a child, I had my own conception of a lady missionary — sweet-faced, gentle creature who moved in an atmosphere of unruffled holiness. The fact that she came from overseas seemed to exempt her from the common strain and stress of life, and I would have been profoundly shocked and disillusioned had I ever heard her utter an irritable word. Fortunately, the specimens who came to stay with us conformed, at least during their visits, to my standards, and it was only much later in life that I began to realise that crossing the seas never made anyone holy. In fact, the moment you enter a foreign country and prepare to attack Satan's strongholds, you are entering a territory of fiercer temptation than ever. You may find weaknesses in yourself that you never suspected at home. If you were touchy, petty, irritable, or self-pitying in England, you will find ten times more opportunity to be so on the mission field after the first feeling of sanctity has worn off. There are spiritual reasons for this, but there are also physical and circumstantial reasons that a prospective candidate would do well to face before ever he embarks on the new life.

Physically and spiritually you are going to work at high pressure, and many of the ordinary means of relaxation and amusement that you enjoyed at home will no longer be available. If you are on a mission centre you will probably have little opportunity to get away from your surroundings, and opportunities for service will always be, so to speak, on your doorstep. The more you truly care, the harder it becomes to relax at all. It is a matter about which one needs to be strong-minded, or the nervous tension of overwork is bound to ensue.

You will probably be very restricted socially. You will no longer be able to choose congenial friends; you must make the best of who you happen to land up with, whether you find each other congenial or not.

When you first arrive you may consider your senior missionary an antiquated bore, and she may consider you a flighty butterfly.

Missionaries as a class are strong characters with strong principles, and perhaps you are too. They may wear outdated fashions and have acquired irritating habits of economy, and it may take you months to appreciate their single-minded devotion to Christ and his work and their true worth. But you cannot often get away from each other, and there is probably very little choice of friends who can speak your language elsewhere, even if you could. Face this problem beforehand and train yourself to mix with different age groups and different types from different backgrounds.

Even if you have nothing else in common, your love for Christ and his work should be enough. But in practice we often fail on this point, and our missionary effort becomes subservient to the effort we are making to live in happy Christian fellowship with that determined old warrior in elastic-sided boots who has just celebrated her fortieth anniversary overseas, or with young "Mr Knowall", aged twenty-four, who just arrived from home last month.

You are having to adapt yourself to new condition. The climate is probably much hotter, and the food much oilier than you like. You may be desperately homesick, and the frustration of being unable to speak the language can be most exhausting.

All these things may result in a slightly lower level of health than you enjoyed before. Medical attention is not quite so easy to come by as at home and your senior missionaries have probably learned to live quite comfortably with their minor ailments.

Tiredness and frustration can turn us into very irritable people at times.

You are longing to represent Christ to a people whose standards and etiquette you as yet know nothing. A serious mistake may establish for you a reputation, which may take you years to live down. Yet you find it hard to go slow and take advice, and you may show annoyance and disgust at things which to them are neither annoying nor disgusting. Many a deep-seated resentment against a missionary has been born in the hearts of the people of the land when the missionary has been quite unconscious of giving offence.

We grow and gain experience rapidly when serving Christ overseas. We look back over past years and shudder at our early self-assurance, our failures and mistakes. If only we'd known and realised… if only we'd seen ourselves as we see ourselves now… if only we'd been more humble! As the increasing light of God's requirements dawns upon us, it is easy to be caught up in a net of shame, discouragement or actual despair. We can't undo the past; we must stay where we are, and live in the circumstance we have built up for ourselves… or else take the easy way, and return home.

Nervous tension, irritability, loneliness, exhaustion, frustration, ignorance, discouragement and depression — the stage is set for all these to attack in their strongest form. And where yielded to, the results are deadly. There must be many a hard-working devoted, self-denying missionary whose joy is blighted and whose power is weakened and whose health is impaired by some secret grudge or resentment, or, far more often, some remorse or deep discouragement, some sense of failure, or some crippling inferiority complex, and the whole list really boils down to one common denominator, a failure to grasp the true meaning of forgiveness. Either we cannot forgive, or we cannot accept forgiveness, or perhaps a mixture of both. And the curious part is that there is so often practically nothing to forgive. Missionaries very seldom engage in open quarrel. They keep perfectly respectable on the surface. The barrier is often built up from a mere look, an imagined slight, or a critical remark repeated third hand at the end of a hot exhausting day.

The only way to understand forgiveness is to look thoughtfully at the nature of the forgiveness of God: *He loves to forgive. 'He delighteth in mercy'* (Micah 7:18). We cherish our grudges and find it hard to be reconciled. It wounds our pride to take the first step, but the Father on the rooftop could not stop himself. He ran to pour out forgiveness on the prodigal; day after day he had been scanning the road yearning for the opportunity to forgive.

His forgiveness always takes the initiative, and our very repentance is the result of his seeking. We say, 'I'm not going to lower myself by running after him, he was in the wrong, and he should come to me,' but God never treats us like that. There is no vestige of pride in the broken-hearted cry, 'I have spread out my hands all day to a rebellious people' (Isaiah 65:2). He did not say of the sheep that had gone astray, 'He's insisted on his own way and spurned all my efforts, I'm through with him until he comes back and apologises.' The Shepherd rose up and took every step of the long road of forgiveness himself, and the sheep never took one to meet him. In fact it never took a step at all. It was carried back on the tide of the Lord's forgiveness.

His forgiveness actively destroys the evil it forgives. It is so strong, so loving, so purifying that it actually cleanses the heart in which it operates, as light scatters darkness, which must surely be the meaning of Matthew 6:15. For if we cannot forgive, then we have shut off a corner of our hearts from the forgiveness of God. Only expose that dark, sullen thought of revenge to the forgiveness of God, and it could no more exist than twilight could exist at sunrise.

His forgiveness forgets. 'Blotted out as a thick cloud... cast into the depths of the sea... removed as far as the East is from the West... cast behind God's back, never to be glanced at again...' these are the expressions used to describe the forgiveness of God. For when God pardons a sinner, he instantly sets him in unclouded, unbroken communion with himself. If the thought of forgiven sin ever comes between God and us again it is because we have remembered, not because God has remembered. But we carry our injuries about with us, and brood on them. We confide them to sympathetic friends, and we indulge in tiny pinpricks of revenge.

His forgiveness sees us through the natural result of our failure. 'I am with thee,' said God to Jacob, 'I will bring thee again' (Genesis 28:15). With him where? Not in the way that God had planned, but in that desert into which he had strayed through his treachery; in the way where the sun had gone down, where he laid his head on a stone and thought himself forsaken.

But he soon learned how wrong he was. The gates of heaven were opened that night and the angels surged forth to compass the lonely path that a repentant sinner had made for himself. But we see one who had failed, reaping the natural consequences, and we inwardly shrug our shoulders. 'After all, he brought it upon himself... he deserves all he gets... If he's not exactly popular, he's asked for it.' Yet it is just at this point that divine forgiveness operates most forcibly. The book of Isaiah tells us that God does not search for new building sites; on the ruins and waste places of our pride and self-confidence he stoops to erect his palaces. 'Thou shalt deny me thrice,' said Christ to Peter, and later on he added, 'I have prayed for thee that thy faith fail not, and when thou art converted, strengthen thy brethren.' The

Lord stood beside him and looked right along the path. He saw the failure, the consequent despair and the tottering faith, the restoration, and the humble restored soul at last usable by God; brought, through failure, to the lowly place where Christ could entrust him with power. Divine forgiveness saw him right through.

Lastly, his forgiveness expresses itself. Many a time, doubt and a sense of strain drag on between two people who both long to be right with each other, because, through shyness or fear or reserve, neither can pluck up the courage to discuss the matter. God, on the other hand, proclaims his forgiveness (Exodus 34:5-7). He knows that our aching hearts need strong reassurance, and he never ties of reiterating in the most vigorous language that all is well. 'Though your sins be as scarlet, they shall be as white as snow… your sins and your iniquities will I remember no more… speak ye comfortably and cry unto her… her iniquity is pardoned.'

'I believe in the forgiveness of sins.' What a revival, and a welling up of love, and strength of unity there would be amongst us if we could truly say that. And also if we were to forgive as we have been forgiven, and accept forgiveness – eagerly, quick to take the first step, willing to forget and to stand by the one who has wronged us until all traces of wrong are blotted out; learning if need be, to break through our reserves and to speak comfortably... 'Forgiving... as God for Christ's sake hath forgiven you.'

I believe in the resurrection

A missionary had just returned from home leave when a younger missionary asked her, 'What did you do when you first got home?'

'Do, my dear?' replied her friend, 'I more or less hid in the kitchen till I could acquire some new clothes. You've no idea what you look like after four years abroad. The fashions and hairstyles nowadays have to be seen to be believed and everything seemed so comfortable and luxurious. Of course, everyone was frightfully kind and piled the best on me, and I enjoyed it all immensely. But sometimes one couldn't help wondering… We seemed to spend so much time and thought on things.'

We certainly live in an age when the cult of the body, its clothing, its adornments and its comfort has reached alarming proportions. The advertisements make more and more fantastic claims, obtruding their maxims on our subconscious minds from every street corner and magazine. According to them true bliss is to be attained through a comfortable mattress, true mother-love is demonstrated by the brand of toilet soap a woman buys; the happiness of your home depends on the softness of your carpet, and the happiness of your marriage on your perfume or your hairspray. Values have been so distorted that our girls can spend hours of their time poring over more than a dozen different shades of lipstick, each with its own seductive name, the right choice of which is alleged to be absolutely essential to the blossoming of their own particular personality. They are growing up in a world where the wave of a curl and the height of a heel or the shade of a cosmetic have become matters of major importance – subjects that can fill their minds to the exclusion of almost everything else.

'Is not the life more than meat, and the body than raiment?' asked Christ.

'The things that are seen are temporal, but the things that are not seen are eternal,' said St Paul.

'Ye... took joyfully the spoiling of your goods, knowing... that ye have in heaven a better and an enduring substance,' said the writer to the Hebrews.

'My dear,' said Jonathan Goforth to his young wife who was bemoaning the loss of her property, 'why do you grieve so? They are only things.'

The young would-be missionary who has grown up in this present age of softness and luxury and self-indulgence does well to stand still, before he ever commits himself to whole-time service to Christ and to take stock of his sense of values. For which world is he really living?

We go out proclaiming that we believe in the resurrection of the body and in the life everlasting, and in this materialistic age it is a new idea to many. The Sermon on the Mount teaches us in the clearest terms that we cannot set out to grasp two worlds. We must concentrate on treasure on earth or treasure in heaven; God or mammon; human standard of blessing or the everlasting state, and we concentrate on one only at the expense of the other.

How very, very carefully the people overseas watch us. We inform them that this body is earthly and this life temporal; that the things, which really matter, are over there on the other side. We have to live in this world, and to do God's work adequately we need to keep healthy, but does anything belie our teaching more than too much care and elegance lavished on the house and garden, too much zealous adherence to our rest and recreation hours? In short, the preservation of a standard of living which, though it may be simple to us, is probably far above the standard of the people amongst whom we live. They say little, but how accurately they assess our attitude, and occasionally the chance remark is dropped which shows how they sum us up.

A missionary, newly out from England, took great pains over the little plot of ground in front of his house; and a pretty patch of flowers replaced the worn mud path over which the women had been used to tramp on their way to the well. He built a fence round his garden, but one day two of them carrying heavy water pots stepped over his enclosure and came plodding right through the little sanctuary. He rush out, thoroughly roused, told them what he thought of them and hustled them off the premises, hoping they had learned their lesson. They had. As he turned away, he heard one of them remark wonderingly to the other, 'But that is the man who preaches to us about love on Sundays!'

What was wrong? Not the flowers. They were a bright patch of beauty for everyone to enjoy. It was his sense of values. His mistake lay in thinking that his so soon fading garden mattered more than the heavy laden women.

I have known the feeling myself when some kindly visitor from the country innocently blows her nose on the covers or contentedly spits on the floor. Suddenly the furniture seems to matter more than the visitor. But the covers will fade in a few years, and we shall never think of them at all over there, while the soul of a country woman won by patient love will shine for ever like a star in the life everlasting.

'We don't mind for ourselves, but we must have things nice for our children,' some will protest. That is true and the child's real wants, spiritual and material must always be a parent's first consideration. But missionaries are doing their children grave wrong if they lead them to believe that the happiness of a home depends on material comfort and plenty. The children are not harmed by being allowed, in some small way, to share their parents' choice of work and the separations and privations involved.

'Why do I have to play with such horrid children?' sobbed a tender-hearted seven-year-old missionary's son after witnessing a display of cruelty and falsehood that to local children was merely amusing.

Any explanation short of the truth may only breed resentment and hatred. There is no answer except the real answer: 'We came here to win these people for Jesus. We could have stayed in England where you could have had nice, good friends; but then these people would never had heard the Gospel. You are part of us. We trust you to be with these children so that you can show them that a Christian child is different.'

The child in this case responded, began to pray for two small boys who had so upset him. A few nights later he was leaning on the windowsill in his pyjamas looking at the stars. 'Look,' he said, pointing at the black patch of the sky. 'That's like the world, isn't it, and those two stars in the middle are like Christians shining for Jesus; the bright part round the moon is like Jesus in heaven… and when I look at the stars they get bigger, like Christians, who shine brighter and brighter until they are almost like Jesus.'

That child had probably begun to understand why his parents had brought him to live in such a black place.

Though I have no statistics at hand, I believe I am right in saying that fewer candidates are applying for overseas mission now than in past years, and this seems strange in the face of the open doors which may close at any moment, plus the increased facilities for travel, and the time is short. What has happened?

Have we, perhaps, lost our true sense of proportion? Have we rated our mortal bodies and our temporal, physical lives at too high a value? Are there any left who would lay wealth, comfort, convenience and earthly affections in the balance and say of them, 'These I counted loss for Christ?' Are there any true successors of those old Moravian missionaries who laid aside their fine clothing and sold themselves as slaves in the slave market and entered the territory, forbidden to missionaries, in lifelong chains and fetters? Are there any who could subscribe to Carey's description: 'The servant of Christ will be ready for hardship, foregoing a numerous auditory, cordial friends, a civilised country, legal protection, affluence, or even a competency, and be prepared for slights, hatred, pretended friends, prisons, tortures, the society of barbarians of uncouth speech, miserable accommodation, hunger, thirst, weariness and painfulness, hard work and little encouragement'?

Few of today's missionaries will ever have to face the physical deprivation and hardships of our forefathers. Our sacrifices will be much smaller and subtler, and our acceptance or refusal of them will probably decide the usefulness and influence of our missionary service. Our attitude to them will depend on our sense of values. Just how important is our mortal body and the things that pertain to

this mortal life? How clearly have we apprehended the reality of the resurrection body and the life everlasting? How much do we look at things in the light of eternity? What practical difference does it make to us? What will it be like when we reach the boundary and look back on the temporal things that loomed so large and seemed so important – in that hour when we are about to abandon them for ever?

A gallant old pioneer missionary lay dead in his brushwood hut in the jungle. On the fly-leaf of his worn Bible were written these words:

> When I am dying how glad I shall be
> That the lamp of my life
> has been burnt out for thee,
> The time that I spent and the labour I gave,
> 'Twill seem nothing if through it
> one soul thou should'st save.
> The way I have trod has been weary and rough,
> But it led to they feet, Lord, and that was enough.
> When I am dying how glad I shall be
> That the lamp of my life
> has been burnt out for thee.

If we can use our possessions and our pretty, tasteful, homes to serve and attract the people we came to win, then let us thank God for them. But the moment we begin grieving and fretting over the wear and tear, and the covers spoiled by the muddy 'brother or sister for whom Christ died', then our sense of proportion has gone astray and we need to ask ourselves afresh, which life do I really believe in? – and which matters most?

May we take our stand once and for all with all those who have ever suffered any loss gladly for Christ's sake, and reply, 'I believe in the life everlasting.'

Aisha's Letter

Old Aisha lived in a village high among the rocks looking out over the Riff Mountains. She had lived in that village all her life and except for an occasional trip to the market, it was the only world she knew.

As a child she had tended the goats high up where the charcoal burners lit their fires among the scrub. As a girl she had later married, and travelled on horseback from the little thatched hut under the oak trees at the top of the village to another thatched hut under the oak trees at the bottom of the village; and here she ground corn and drew water everyday of her life, and here she had borne and brought up her children. But now her husband had died and her children had married and gone off to other villages, so old Aisha was left alone.

She was troubled because she seemed to be going blind, and whatever would happen to her then? Her daughters loved her but her sons-in-law did not want her in their homes, and besides, her own little home was dear to her. Perhaps something could be done about her eyesight. That night when her neighbours came back from the market, she tackled them on the subject.

They were quite encouraging.

Yes, there was a missionary nurse in the little market town, and she had good medicine.

Many went there and were cured of coughs and spots and sore eyes.

No, she did not ask for money.

Yes, old Aisha should certainly go.

They would take her on the mule when they next went to town.

Aisha went home comforted, sure that her sight would be restored.

A week later Aisha sat in the small mission dispensary, peering round and waiting her turn. When it came, the nurse greeted her kindly, examined her eyes and told her to sit down again. When all the other patients had gone the nurse came and talked to her alone in her own language, and this was such a surprise to Aisha that it was quite a long time before she found herself able to listen to anything she said. But at last they found themselves communicating:

"I can't do anything for your eyes," said the nurse. "You need an operation. But my brother in the town on the coast is an eye doctor. I think he could make you see."

"But how would I get to him?"

"In the bus."

"But I've never been in the long distance buses and I have no money."

"Perhaps your children would help you?"

"But if I did, what would I do when I got there?

I've never been in the town and I would get lost."

"You must ask your way to the hospital. Everyone knows the hospital."

"And if I did get there, the doctor might not let me in. I'm only a poor old woman, and he won't fully understand my language."

"He sees many poor old women every day, and he speaks your language. Besides, I will give you a letter telling him that you come from far."

The idea of a letter seemed to comfort her. She went back to the village and got in touch with her children.

One day she arrived with her son-in-law who was going to buy her a ticket and put her on a bus, and another distant relative would meet her and lodge her. But she wanted that letter. She had great faith in that letter.

It was quite a long time before the nurse saw her again, and when at last she turned up she was hardly recognisable for she wore spectacles and walked confidently. The shuffling feet and the peering look had quite changed. She could see. She arrived again in the middle of the dispensary, but again she waited until all had gone for she had a story to tell. So the nurse took her upstairs and, over a glass of mint tea, Aisha recounted her experiences, and the nurse smiled, imagining the scene – the busy outpatients department, the crowds at the door, the harassed doctor and the determined old woman.

"I went up early in the morning, as you said," began Aisha, "and as I said, I got lost. The relative with whom I stayed gave me money for the bus, but I got the wrong one and it was the time of the second prayer call when I arrived. The door was shut and there were many standing outside, late like me, and they knocked at that shut door.

"But the doorkeeper came out and told us that the room was full, and we must all go away and come back in the afternoon, or the next day. No one else could come in. The people argued and some were angry, but it was no use. The door was shut.

"But I held up my letter and I shouted in a loud voice, 'but I come in the name of his sister; I come in the name of his sister.'"

The doorkeeper glanced at the letter. It seemed authentic and, for all he knew, it might be urgent. He admitted her and took her to the consulting room, and the doctor, recognising the writing, read the letter at once and glanced at her eyes.

The condition was obvious and he told her that he would admit her at once. It was all a perfectly ordinary routine event, but to her it had seemed wonderful.

"The doorkeeper beckoned me in," she continued with shining eyes, "I alone! All the others had to go away. There were many waiting but he led me through the crowds in front of them all into the presence of the doctor. And I said again, 'I come in the name of your sister.' Many were waiting but he turned from them and took the letter from me and read it right there. And then he turned to me, who am old and poor, and he did for me all that you asked – a bed, an operation … and now I can see."

She paused and considered. When she spoke again her voice was soft and wondering. "How precious is your name to him," she murmured. "He did for me all that you asked. How precious is your name."

"*In the name of Jesus*," *is not a magic formula to have our prayers answered. As we have seen, it is Jesus' life, death and resurrection that have brought us back to God. It is because of what Jesus has done that we are again acceptable to God and can come to him through prayer. It is therefore through faith in Jesus, because of our belief in him, that our prayers are heard.*

By praying "in Jesus' name," we are simply acknowledging to God, and reminding ourselves, that we owe our new relationship with God entirely to Jesus and his work.

It also means that, just as the nurse asked for certain things for Aisha by letter, signed in her name, so we can ask and receive anything the Lord wants us to have, and this includes everything that he has promised us in the Bible

Theme:

Prayer in the name of Jesus

Bible Passage:

John 16:23-27

Scripture verses:

Jesus … lives forever to plead with God for them.

Hebrews 7:25

And so he Jesus is able, now and always, to save those who come to God through him.

Hebrews 7:25

I am telling you the truth: the Father will give you anything you ask him for in my name.

John 16:23.

Patricia St John
- her story -
written by Irene Howat

Patricia wanted to hear one of her favourite stories. 'Please tell me again about when I was born,' she asked.

Mrs. St. John laughed. 'You know it so well you could write a book about it.'

The six-year-old grinned.

'Please ....'

'All right then,' her mother agreed. 'Dad and I were missionaries in Brazil. We loved it there, despite our home being aptly nicknamed 'The House of a Thousand Fleas.' However, Dad was asked to set up Bible schools in remote villages, which would have meant a life of travelling. That was why he went back alone and I stayed here in England with your sister and brother.'

'But you've missed out me being born!'

'Oops. Right! In 1919, not long before Dad returned to Brazil alone, he borrowed a pram big enough to take both your sister and brother. He wasn't used to pushing a pram. It ran out of control and Hazel and Farnham were thrown out. They weren't hurt, but I got such a fright that you were born a few hours later.'

Patricia grinned. 'What a start!'

'Write a story about home,' the teacher said. 'Just a few sentences.'

Patricia St. John picked up her pencil.

'Home is called Homesdale and it's in Malvern. Great Granny lives there, and Granny and Mum. Then there's my big sister Hazel and my big brother Farnham, and me. Dad is a missionary in Brazil and only lives with us when he comes to England. We laugh a lot in our home.'

Mrs. St. John laughed very heartily one day when Patricia's younger brother Oliver was about four.

Oliver had made a pretend train with three chairs, one in front of the other. When she came home, the train had Oliver on the front chair driving and Great Granny in her nightgown on the second. Both were bumping up and down saying, 'Puff, puff, puff'.

'Why are there no other children in our church?' Patricia asked. 'Apart from the Stayputs?'

Granny shook her head. 'You mustn't call those dears the Stayputs. They're so good when they come to church when they're here on holiday.'

The girl nodded. 'That's why we call them the Stayputs. Their hats are always straight on and they never move during the service.'

'Unlike you?' suggested Granny.

'I love church, but I need to move sometimes. And I love Sunday afternoons.'

Smiling, Granny agreed that Sunday afternoons were special.

'Mind you, I don't know how your mother finds time to make these wonderful missionary scrapbooks for you to look at on Sundays.'

'I like our Sunday biscuits,' Patricia said. 'I'm sure there's not another family in England that has

Sunday biscuits made in the shape of the letters of the alphabet so that the children can make them into Bible verses.'

After a Sunday story about a little Chinese girl who learned the verse 'Fear not, I have redeemed you; I have called you by name; you are mine' (Isaiah 43:2), Patricia prayed a special prayer. Kneeling down beside her bed, she told God, 'My name is Patricia, and if you are really calling me I want to come and be yours.'

'Look!' she shouted in delight the following morning. 'What beautiful flowers!'

Having become God's child the little girl saw, even more clearly than before, what a beautiful world her Lord had made.

In 1926 Mrs. St. John took her young family to Switzerland for a year.

'I won't understand what anyone says,' said Patricia, as she set off on her first day at school.

'You'll learn French quickly,' her mother assured her. 'And you'll make friends too.'

She was right. All her life Patricia was a noticing person. She noticed little details and was able to remember them. So, many years later when she wrote *Treasures of the Snow*, she was able to remember details from that year in Switzerland.

Although Patricia had asked the Lord to be her Saviour when she was six, and despite being brought up in a loving Christian home, she was not always a happy teenager. Much of the reason was that her love for the Lord had grown cold. One day, after an angry outburst, Patricia stormed to her room. She was in her mid teens at the time. Picking up an old Bible that she'd rarely read for some years, she opened it.

'Behold, I stand at the door and knock,' she read from Revelation 3:20, 'if any man hear my voice and open the door, I will come in.'

'It was wonderful,' she told her best friend the next day. 'I seemed to see Jesus standing in a storm saying, "If you will ask me in, I will take you where you want to go."'

Patricia wasn't immediately a happy, carefree teenager, but things began to get better as she read her Bible and prayed to her Lord. But there were always some things that could make her smile.

'What's that noise?' a visitor asked one day.

Patricia's mother was on her feet immediately and on her way to the door.

The girl giggled. 'I think we have unwelcome visitors,' she explained. 'We have ducks down at the end of the orchard. If they see our front door open they march up in single file and come in.'

'What do they do then?' she was asked.

'Well, either Mum chases them out again or they march right through the house and go out the back door.' She laughed at the sounds from the hall, 'It's a Mum chasing them day!'

After school Patricia had hoped to study medicine like her older brother. Unfortunately there was a mix-up with her application form that prevented her from going.

'You can work for me,' her aunt, who ran a school, suggested.

'Helping to teach primary children is not exactly what I want to do,' the girl thought. However, she discovered she enjoyed it very much indeed, even though the job was only a stopgap.

'I've been accepted for nursing training,' she

told her aunt in 1942. 'I'm starting at St. Thomas's Hospital in London next January.

'What a battle-axe,' Patricia thought, after only two days on the ward. 'I'll never be able to please that Sister.'

'Do this quickly! Do that immediately! Do the other thing yesterday!' barked the Sister, all day, every day.

'Oh, my poor fingers,' moaned the young nurse. 'One of them's gone septic.'

Not long afterwards some of her toes became septic too.

'What happening to me?' she asked herself. 'I'm falling apart!'

After a spell off work, Matron suggested she might not be cut out for nursing.

In a fit of despair Patricia went for a walk, eventually arriving at the railway station. There at the entrance, in huge black letters, she read the words, 'Jesus said, "Do you not believe that I am able to do this?"'

Standing in front of the large poster for a long time, the young woman thought hard.

'Yes,' she decided. 'I believe you are able.'

Walking back to the hospital she continued her nursing and did well. When she completed her training, Patricia went home and worked for a local doctor before becoming housemother at her aunt's school.

'You know,' she told her friend. 'So many of these children have missionary parents and they don't see them for years at a time.'

'Do you mother them then?'

Patricia smiled. 'Over the winter months I light a fire in the evenings and the children come down in dressing gowns, clutching their teddy bears, and I tell them a story while they're having their cocoa and biscuits.'

That was the beginning of her storytelling. It was then that she wrote *The Tanglewoods' Secret*. She wrote it, first and foremost, for the children at Clarendon School.

In 1949 Patricia packed her cases and went to be with her brother, a doctor in Tangier, Morocco. For the next year she kept house for him and helped in the hospital. Then the time came when the Lord led her to work in a mountain town above Tangier.

'My little house has a wonderful view,' she wrote home. 'I look down on the marketplace, then over layers of many roofs to the mountains. Mind you, it does have some disadvantages. Yesterday my room flooded again and I came home to find my saucepan bobbing along like a boat in full sail. Time to go – must get on with my language study.'

And that's what kept Patricia busy for her first few months there, that and completing *Treasures of the Snow*.

'Hello,' she said when she opened her door one day.

'I'm hungry. Can I have some bread?'

Patricia looked at the thin little lad on her doorstep.

'Of course, come in and have some.'

The following night he arrived with five or six of his friends. They'd never tasted bread and treacle before, and they loved it.

'Would you like me to tell you a story?' Patricia asked, as they licked their fingers.

They grinned and said they would. She told them about Jesus, the Good Shepherd. Bread and treacle with a story was a recipe that kept the boys coming back. Wherever she went, Patricia reached right to the heart of children, usually through her stories.

'Goodness me,' laughed Patricia, as she unpacked a parcel one day. 'A clockwork mouse!'

It had come from someone who had heard about the children. The boys and girls loved it, and they were not the only ones.

'Thank you for coming,' the missionary said to the ladies who had attended her meeting.

Nobody moved and more women started to appear. Patricia gave another talk and again thanked the women for coming. No one moved. Puzzled, she waited for an explanation.

'We've come to see the mouse,' admitted one of the ladies.

Greatly amused Patricia took out the clockwork mouse, wound it up, and watched as her visitors screamed at its antics.

'That's one way to encourage women to come to meetings,' she thought, when they did eventually go. 'And they heard two talks about Jesus.'

When winter drew on, and children kept coming

to her home for stories, Patricia started to write *Star of Light*, based on what she saw around her then.

'Would you come and visit the sick people in our village?' she was asked after a while.

'Yes,' replied Patricia, delighted to have the opportunity to help and to talk about the Lord Jesus Christ.

'Now then,' she said to her helper. 'What do we need?'

Patricia went through a list, 'Iron tablets, malt for mums-to-be, eye ointment and worm medicines, sulphur tablets for babies who have sickness and diarrhoea. What else?'

'Do you have the gentian violet for sores?'

'What would I do without you?' Patricia smiled, popping the gentian violet into her bag.

When she was asked to stay overnight in villages there was more storytelling.

Five years after moving to town, the missionary work began to be opposed.

'There have been complaints about your activities,' she was told. 'And I'm afraid we're cancelling your helper's visa.'

Patricia was not the only one who was broken-hearted at the thought of leaving the town. She left many sad friends behind, adults as well as children, but they still remembered her stories. However, as she travelled to England for Christmas she thought over her work in Morocco and smiled. As well as teaching and nursing she'd written *Three Go Searching*, *The Fourth Candle* and *Star of Light*.

When Patricia returned to Morocco, it was to Tangier where Farnham was a doctor.

'You attract young people,' her brother said, when she set up home with seven teenage girls, all of them student nurses.

'What do I do?' she wrote home in answer to a letter. 'I teach the girls, help look after them, and child-mind for Farnham and Janet's six children when I can. As well as that I help at the baby milk clinic, do what I can in the hospital – and tell stories to anyone who will listen. It's a busy life!'

Patricia's life certainly was busy. In 1966 she left Morocco to go to Rwanda in order to research a book on the history of a period of church growth known as the Rwanda Revival. For some years God blessed Rwanda in an amazing way and Patricia was asked to write a book about it. Of course, her time in Rwanda made her long for revival in her beloved Morocco, that Muslim land in which teaching about Jesus was often far from welcome.

'I've always been fascinated by the story of Onesimus in the Bible,' Patricia told a friend.

'Why don't you write about him then?' was the reply.

'I can't,' explained the storyteller. 'I can only write about places I've been to.'

'Then go!'

That was the start of a trip round Bible sites that enabled her to write *Twice Freed*, the story of Onesimus, the runaway slave.

'I can hardly believe that it's ten years since I wrote about Onesimus,' said Patricia to her sister Hazel in 1976. 'Or that I'm back in the Middle East. What a busy city Beirut is.'

She had gone to help Hazel for a few weeks after she'd fractured her hip in a fall.

'You're doing well on those crutches,' Patricia laughed. 'In fact, you're hopping around like a kangaroo. It won't be long until you'll be well enough to wave me goodbye and send me back to England.'

'No doubt you'll put this visit to good use and write a book based on what you've seen.'

Her younger sister laughed. 'You never know.'

She did. It's called *Nothing Else Matters*.

Patricia's life proclaimed the fact that nothing else does matter - but Christ. And on her death in November 1993, Patricia St. John met Christ face to face. It is amazing to think of how in heaven she met the one whose stories she had known and loved since before she could remember.

Bible Passages to Read

*I believe in God the Father Almighty,
creator of Heaven and Earth*

Genesis 1: 26-31

Genesis 3

Luke 15:11-32

Ephesians 2:12, 18

Psalm 8.

*I believe in Jesus Christ,
his only Son, Our Lord*

Job 42:1-6

Isaiah 6, 53

Matthew 28:1-10

Luke 15

John 1:1-13, 3:1-16; 13:1-13, 20:1-23

Romans 5:6-21

2 Corinthians 5:14-21

Hebrews 1:1-2, 2:9-18

1 Peter 2:21-25

1 John 1.

I believe in the Holy Spirit

John 14:15-23, 14:27, 16:20-33
Romans 8:1-11
2 Corinthians 3:18, 4:1-6; 5:14-21
Galatians 5
Colossians 3:1-4
1 John 3:1-3.

I believe in the communion of saints, the forgiveness of sins

Psalm 11, 27, 31:1-5, 91
Malachi 3:10
Matthew 10:16-42
John 16:23-27
Romans 8:28, 10:6-18
1 Corinthians 12; 2 Corinthians 5:14-21
1 John 1.

I believe in the resurrection of the body and the life everlasting

Matthew 24:32-51
John 14:3
1 Corinthians 15
Revelation 22:20

Ten Girls who used their Talents

by Irene Howat

The biography chapter of Patricia St. John has been taken from the book: Ten Girls who used their talents.

Writers, medics, missionaries and bus drivers are all included in this book. These are the stories of ten girls who grew up to use their gifts and talents to honour God. Patricia St. John had many gifts - she had a gift for healing, for caring, for helping people as well as for writing. Patricia used all these gifts to spread the good news of Jesus Christ.

Names included in this book: Harriet Beecher Stowe; Mildred Cable; Sarah Edwards; Annie Lawson; Maureen McKenna; Katie Ann Mackinnon; Selina Countess of Huntingdon, Helen Roseveare, Patricia St. John, Mary Verghese.

ISBN: 978-1-84550-147-1

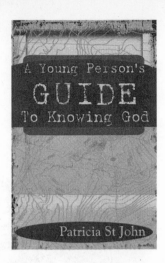

A Young Person's Guide to Knowing God
by Patricia St. John

Patricia St. John's gift for storytelling was second to none. In this book she weaves together stories like Aisha's Letter and others to bring to life the truths of the Apostles' Creed and scripture. Every chapter deals with a basic Christian belief and tackles some of the most searching questions the author was asked, including:

Who is God and what is he like? Why is there so much suffering in the world? Wasn't I born a Christian? Does Jesus care about me? Can I really know God?

Through enjoyable real-life stories, prayers and thought-provoking questions, the reader will discover what Christians believe and what friendship with Jesus can mean in their lives.

ISBN: 9781857925586

Twice Freed
by Patricia St. John

This is a well known and well loved fictional story written by Patricia St. John. It is based on the biblical narrative of Onesimus and Philemon. Onesimus, a slave in the 1st Century A.D. is a very discontented young man. He doesn't want anything to do with God, Jesus Christ or this Paul who keeps stirring things up. Onesimus longs for freedom to live his own life so as soon as the opportunity arises he runs away from his master. This is the beginning of a series of thrilling and dangerous adventures for the young man. However, as he does his utmost to run away from his life and responsibilities he is also trying to run away from God.

ISBN: 9781857924893

Counsel for Christian Workers
by C.H. Spurgeon

C. H. Spurgeon's sermons drew thousands to his church and, when printed, sold in their millions. A hundred years later he is still one of the most popular Christian authors in print. Yet, at the heart of Spurgeon's desire to preach was a love of people.

His concern extended particularly to those involved in Christian ministry. 'Counsel for Christian Workers' was produced for those involved in a variety of Christian work. They contain Spurgeon's clear sighted and pithy analysis and viewpoints on the issues that face such people.

Spurgeon was essentially a practical and loving man and this shines through the pages of this collection of his teaching. Here is wisdom that will continue to help Christian workers achieve greater things in their ministry.

ISBN: 9781857926521

CHRISTIAN FOCUS PUBLICATIONS

Christian Focus | Christian Heritage | CF4K | Mentor

Christian Focus Publications publishes books for adults and children under its three main imprints: Christian Focus, Mentor and Christian Heritage. Our books reflect that God's word is reliable and Jesus is the way to know him, and live for ever with him.

Our children's publication list includes a Sunday school curriculum that covers pre-school to early teens; puzzle and activity books. We also publish personal and family devotional titles, biographies and inspirational stories that children will love.

If you are looking for quality Bible teaching for children then we have an excellent range of Bible story and age specific theological books.

From pre-school to teenage fiction, we have it covered!

Find us at our web page:
www.christianfocus.com

CF4•K
Because you're never
too young to know Jesus